ISBN : 0-89898-156-5
Copyright © 1982, 1990 CPP/Belwin, Inc.
15800 N.W. 48th Avenue, Miami, Florida 33014

CREEDENCE CLEARWATER REVIVAL

BAD MOON RISING 4
BEFORE YOU ACCUSE ME 98
BOOTLEG 46
BORN ON THE BAYOU 83
BORN TO MOVE 130
CHAMELEON 24
COMMOTION 116
COTTON FIELDS 96
CROSS-TIE WALKER 34
DON'T LOOK NOW 157
DOOR TO DOOR 67
DOWN ON THE CORNER 128
EFFIGY 15
FEELIN' BLUE 114
FORTUNATE SON 94
GET DOWN WOMAN 56
GLOOMY 30
GOOD GOLLY MISS MOLLY 145
GRAVEYARD TRAIN 132
GREEN RIVER 64

HAVE YOU EVER SEEN THE RAIN? 148
HELLO MARY LOU 22
HEY, TONIGHT 163
(Wish I Could) HIDEAWAY 110
I HEARD IT THROUGH THE GRAPEVINE 169
I PUT A SPELL ON YOU 61
IT CAME OUT OF THE SKY 77
IT'S JUST A THOUGHT 142
KEEP ON CHOOGLIN' 32
LODI 92
LONG AS I CAN SEE THE LIGHT 80
LOOKIN' FOR A REASON 166
LOOKIN' OUT MY BACK DOOR 44
(THE) MIDNIGHT SPECIAL 118
MOLINA 154
MY BABY LEFT ME 126
NEED SOMEONE TO HOLD 39
(THE) NIGHT TIME IS THE RIGHT TIME 74
NINETY-NINE AND A HALF WON'T DO · 139
OOBY DOOBY 90
PAGAN BABY 9
PENTHOUSE PAUPER 124
POORBOY SHUFFLE 51
PORTERVILLE 72
PROUD MARY 108
RAMBLE TAMBLE 27
(Theme From) RUDE AWAKENING NO. 2 160
RUN THROUGH THE JUNGLE 58
SAIL AWAY 100
SAILOR'S LAMENT 6
SIDE O' THE ROAD 136
SINISTER PURPOSE 88
SOMEDAY NEVER COMES 48
SUSIE-Q 54
SWEET HITCH-HIKER 70
TAKE IT LIKE A FRIEND 18
TEARIN' UP THE COUNTRY 103
TOMBSTONE SHADOW 134
TRAVELIN' BAND 36
UP AROUND THE BEND 121
WALK ON THE WATER 86
WHAT ARE YOU GONNA DO 12
WHO'LL STOP THE RAIN 151
(THE) WORKING MAN 106
WROTE A SONG FOR EVERYONE 42

Lettering: STEVE KNEIPP/Editor: AUDREY L. KLEINER

BAD MOON RISING

J.C. FOGERTY

Bad Moon Rising - 2 - 1

SAILOR'S LAMENT

J.C. FOGERTY

Sailor's Lament - 3 - 1

PAGAN BABY

J.C. FOGERTY

10

WHAT ARE YOU GONNA DO

D. CLIFFORD

When you are a-lone, ___ you come ___ back ___ cry-in' and you

want to go home; ___ For some-one for-get-tin' it seems ___ like you're let-tin' it take ___

___ you a-way ___ from me. ___

Was your i-dea to pack ___
Told you all the se-
Thought that I was all ___

_____ up and go. ___
- crets that were mine. ___
_____ that you need, ___

You said you had ___ no
The good things that I
You told me things I

What Are You Gonna Do - 3 - 1

14

What Are You Gonna Do - 3-3

EFFIGY

J.C. FOGERTY

Last night__ I saw a fi - re burn-ing on the pal-ace lawn.__

O'er the land__ the hum-ble sub-jects watched in mixed

e - mo-tion. Who is burn-in'? Who is burn-in'?

Effigy - 3 - 1

```
Subject: TAB: Roadhouse Blues - the Doors
From: The Loan Arranger
Date: Tue, Oct 14, 1997 19:31 EDT
Message-id:

    Roadhouse Blues

Doors
"The Doors"


         Performance Notes
   Play as a shuffle rhythm


e------------------------|------------------------|
b------------------------|------------------------|
g------------------------|------------------------|
d------------------------|---------------0h1h2-|
a-----------------0h1h2-|------------------------|
e-0--0--0--0--0--0-------|-0--0--0--0--0--0-------|

e------------------------|------------------------|
b------------------------|------------------------|
g------------------------|------------------------|
d------------------------|---------------0h1h2-|
a-----------------0h1h2-|------------------------|
e-0--0--0--0--0--0-------|-0--0--0--0--0--0-------|

e----------------------|----------------------|
b----------------------|----------------------|
g----------------------|----------------------|
d----------------------|---------------0h1/2-|
a----------------------|----------------------|
e-0--0--0--0--0--0--3/4-|-0--0--0--0--0--0-------|

e------------------------|------------------------|
b------------------------|------------------------|
g------------------------|------------------------|
d------------------------|---------------0h1h2-|
a-----------------0h1h2-|------------------------|
e-0--0--0--0--0--0-------|-0--0--0--0--0--0-------|

e------------------------|------------------------|
b------------------------|------------------------|
g------------------------|------------------------|
d-----------------0h1h2-|---------------0h1h2-|
a------------------------|------------------------|
e-0--0--0--0--0--0-------|-0--0--0--0--0--0-------|

e-----------------------|------------------------|
b-----------------------|------------------------|
g-----------------------|------------------------|
d-----------------------|---------------0h1h2--|
a-----------------0h1h2-|------------------------|
e-0--0--0--0--0--0-------|-0--0--0--0--0--0--------|
                                    Ah keep your

e-----------------------|------------------------|
b-----------------------|------------------------|
g-----------------------|------------------------|
d---------------0h1h2-|------------------------|
a-----------------------|---------------0h1h2-|
```

```
e-0--0--0--0--0--0---------|-0--0--0--0--0--0--------|
  eyes on the road your hand     upon the wheel
```

```
e-----------------------|--------------------------|
b-----------------------|--------------------------|
g-----------------------|-0------------------------|
d------------------0h1h2-|--------2-0h2--(2)p0-----0----|
a-----------------------|--------------------2-----2-|
e-0--0--0--0--0--0--------|--------------------------|
                                     Ah keep your
```

```
e-----------------------|--------------------------|
b-----------------------|--------------------------|
g-----------------------|--------------------------|
d-----------------------|----------------0h1h2-|
a------------------0h1h2-|--------------------------|
e-0--0--0--0--0--0--------|-0--0--0--0--0--0--------|
  eyes on the road and yer  hand    upon    the wheel
```

```
e-----------------------|--------------------------|
b-----------------------|--------------------------|
g-----------------------|--0-----------------------|
d------------------0h1h2-|--0--2--0h2-(2)p0-----0----|
a-----------------------|--------------------2-----2-|
e-0--0--0--0--0--0--------|--------------------------|
                                     Yeah we're
```

```
e-----------------------|--------------------------|
b-----------------------|--------------------------|
g-----------------------|--------------------------|
d-0-----0-----0--------2--|-----2-----0-------0-------|
a----2-----2-----2--------|-------------2-----------|
e-----------------------|--------------------3--|
  going to the roadhouse     gonna have a real
```

```
e-----------------------|--------------------------|
b-----------------------|--------------------------|
g-----------------------|-0------------------------|
d-----------------------|------2--0h2-(2)p0-----0---|
a------------------0h1h2-|--------------------2------|
e-------0--0------------|--------------------------|
   F^&%&^%    good time
BTW: Is it just me or does he swear here?
```

```
e----------0---------------|-------------------------|
b----3-----3---------------|----3------3--3----------|
g-X--1-----1---------------|----1------1--1----------|
d-X--2-----2--------0----|----2------2--2------0h1h2--|
a-X--------2-------------|-------------------------|
e---------------0--------|-0-----------------------|
  P.M.--|      P.M.       P.M.           P.M.--|
```

```
e----0-----0---------------|-----------0-------------|
b----3-----3---------------|----3------3-------------|
g----1-----1---------------|----1------1-------------|
d----2-----2--------0h1--|----2------2---------0h1h2--|
a-------------------------|-------------------------|
e-0-------------0--------|-0-----------------0-------|
  P.M.                              Yeah at the
```

```
e-----------------------|--------------------------|
b----3------3-----------|----3------3--------------|
g----1------1-----------|----1------1--------------|
d----2------2------0h1h2---|----2------2---------0h1h2--|
```

```
a------------------------|------------------------|
e-0----------------------|-0----------------------|
  back of the road house they got some bungalows
```

```
e------------------------|------------------------|
b----3----3--------------|------------------------|
g----1----1--------------|-0----------------------|
d----2----2----X----0h1h2-|-----2-0h2----0-----0-----|
a---------------2--------|----------------2-----2--|
e-0----------------------|------------------------|
                                         Yeah at the
```

```
e------------------------|------------------------|
b----3------3------------|----3------3------------|
g----1------1------------|----1------1------------|
d----2------2-----0h1h2---|----2------2---------0------|
a------------------------|------------------------|
e-0-----------0----------|-0----------------------|
    back of the roadhouse they got   some    bungalows
```

```
e----------0-------------|------------------------|
b----3------3------------|------------------------|
g----1------1------------|-0----------------------|
d----2------2------------|-----2-0h2-(2)p0-----0-----|
a--------------0h2-0h1h2-|----------------2-----2--|
e-0----------------------|------------------------|
                                              And
```

```
e------------------------|------------------------|
b------------------------|------------------------|
g------------------------|------------------------|
d-0-----0-----0-----0h2--|(2)/\-2--0--0---------0------|
a----2-----2-----2-------|--------------2-----------|
e------------------------|---------------------3--|
  that's for the people who like to go down       slow
```

```
e--------------------------|----------------------|
b--------------------------|----------------------|
g--------------------------|-0--------------------|
d--------------------------|--------2-0h2----(2)/-|
a-----------------0h1h2-|----------------------|
e-(3)/\/\/\--0--0-----0-------|----------------------|
                                              Let it
```

```
e--------------------|----------------------|
b--------------------|----------------------|
g-2------------------|----------------------|
d-2----------2-----4--2-|-2----------2-----4--2--|
a-0--0--3--4--0--0-----0-|-0--0--3--4--0--0-----0--|
e--------------------|----------------------|
    P.M.----|  PM   PM   P.M.----|  PM   PM
  roll   baby   roll                Let it
```

```
e--------------------|----------------------|
b--------------------|----------------------|
g-2------------------|----------------------|
d-2----------2-----4--2-|-2----------2-----4--2--|
a-0--0--3--4--0--0-----0-|-0--0--3--4--0--0-----0--|
e--------------------|----------------------|
    P.M.----|  PM   PM   P.M.----|  PM   PM
  roll   baby   roll                Let it roll
```

```
e----------------------|----------------------|
b----------------------|----------------------|
```

```
g-2--------------------|----------------------|
d-2-----------2-----4--2-|-2-----------2-----4-----|
a-0--0--3--4--0--0-----0-|-0--0--3--4--0--0--------|
e--------------------|----------------------|
     P.M.----|  PM   PM    P.M.----|  PM
   baby   roll                        Let it
```

```
   3     3     3     3        3
   _____ _____ _____ _____    _____
e-----------------------|-----------------------|
b-4-4-4-4-4-4-4-4-4-4-4-4-|-5---5---5---4-------------|
g-4-4-4-4-4-4-4-4-4-4-4-4-|-5---5---5---4-------------|
d-4-4-4-4-4-4-4-4-4-4-4-4-|-5---5---5---4-------------|
a-2-2-2-2-2-2-2-2-2-2-2-2-|-3---3---3---2-------------|
e-----------------------|-----------------------|
   roll                     all night long
```

```
        Guitar Solo
   3           3        3          3
   _____ _____ _____ _____
e-12-12-12-12-12-12-12-12-12-----12-12-|
b-12-12-12-12-12-12-12-12-12---)-12-12-|
g--------------------------14--------|
d-----------------------------------|
a-----------------------------------|
e-----------------------------------|
```

```
    3        3        3        3
   _____ _____ _____ _____
e-----------------------------12--------12-|
b---)-12-12-12---)-12-12---)-12-12---)-12-12-|
g-14-----------14--------14--------14--------|
d-----------------------------------|
a-----------------------------------|
e-----------------------------------|
          Do it Robbie!!  Do It !!
```

```
    3        3           3        3
   _____ _____ _____ _____
e--------12-----------------------------|
b---)-12-12---)-12---)-12---)---12---)-12------)-|
g-14--------14-----14-----14-------14-----14-12--|
d-----------------------------------|
a-----------------------------------|
e-----------------------------------|
```

```
    3         3        3
   _____ _____ _____
               | ̄|--|              )
e-------------------12----------)-15--|
b---)-12---)-12-12-----15-12-14)-----|
g-14-----14-------------------14------|
d-----------------------------------|
a-----------------------------------|
e-----------------------------------|
```

```
          6
          _____
e(15)-15-12---)-12----12-12---)----12---12--|
b-----------15-----15-------15-------------|
g-----------------------------------|
d-----------------------------------|
a-----------------------------------|
```

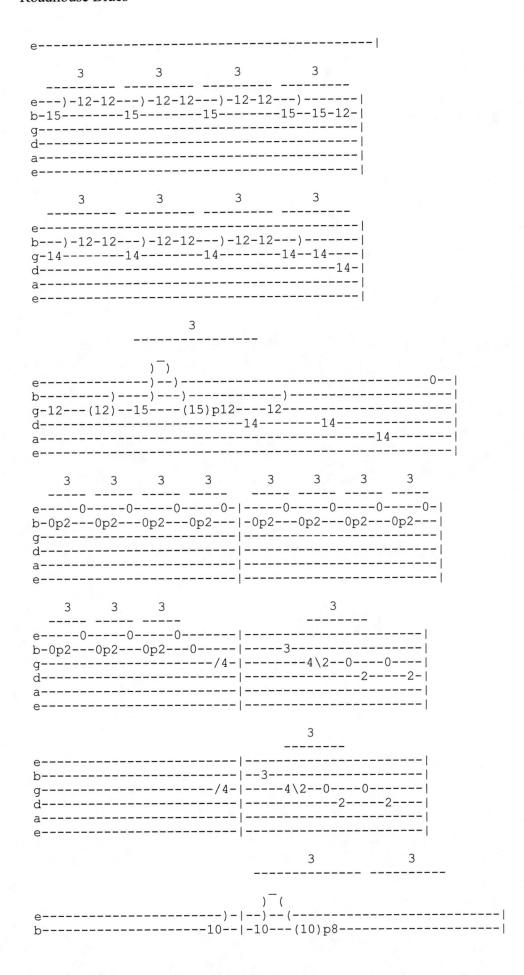

```
g-----------------------------|-----------------9-<7>-<7>--0-------|
d-----------------------------|------------------------------0----|
a-----------------------------|------------------------------2-|
e-----------------------------|------------------------------|
```

```
e-----------------------------|-----------------------------|
b-----------------------------|-----------------------------|
g-----------------------------|-----------------------------|
d----2--X--2--2---------------|----2--X--2--2--2------------|
a--------------2--0h1h2-|-------------------0h1h2---|
e-0---------------------------|-0---------------------------|
  PM                   You got to roll, roll, roll, you gotta
```

```
e-----------------------------|-----------------------------|
b-----------------------------|-----------------------------|
g-----------------------------|-----------------------------|
d----2-----2--2--2--0----|----2--2--2--2--2--0-----|
a--------------------2-|------------------2--|
e-0--------------------------|-0---------------------------|
 thrill my soul alright   PM                      PM
```

```
e-----------------------------|-----------------------------|
b-----------------------------|-----------------------------|
g-----------------------------|-----------------------------|
d----2-----2-----2--0----|----2-----2-----2--X------|
a--------------------2-|-----------------------2---|
e-0-----0-----0----------|-0-----0-----0-----------|
  PM    PM    PM          PM---------------------|
              Roll roll roll rolla thrill my soul
```

```
e-----------------------------|-----------------------------|
b-----------------------------|-----------------------------|
g-----------------------------|-----------------------------|
d----2-----2-----2--0----|----2-----2--2--2---------|
a--------------------2-|------------------0h1h2--|
e-0--------------------------|-0---------------------------|
  PM                     PM---------------------|
Lyrical scat----------------------------------------
```

```
e-----------------------------|-----------------------------|
b-----------------------------|-----------------------------|
g-----------------------------|-----------------------------|
d----2--X--2--2--2--0----|----2--2---------2--0----|
a--------------------2-|---------------------2-|
e-0--------------------------|-0---------------------------|
  PM                     PM----|
----------------------------------------------
```

```
e-----------------------------|-----------------------------|
b-----------------------------|-----------------------------|
g-----------------------------|-----------------------------|
d----0-----2--2--2--0----|----2-----2--2--2---------|
a--------------------2-|------------------0h1h2--|
e-0--------------------------|-0---------------------------|
         PM---------------|
--------------------------------------- Yeah
```

```
e-----------------------------|-----------------------------|
b-----------------------------|-----------------------------|
g-----------------------------|-----------------------------|
d----2-----2--2--2--0----|----2--2--2--2--2--0----|
a--------------------2-|---------------------2-|
e-0--------------------------|-0---------------------------|
```

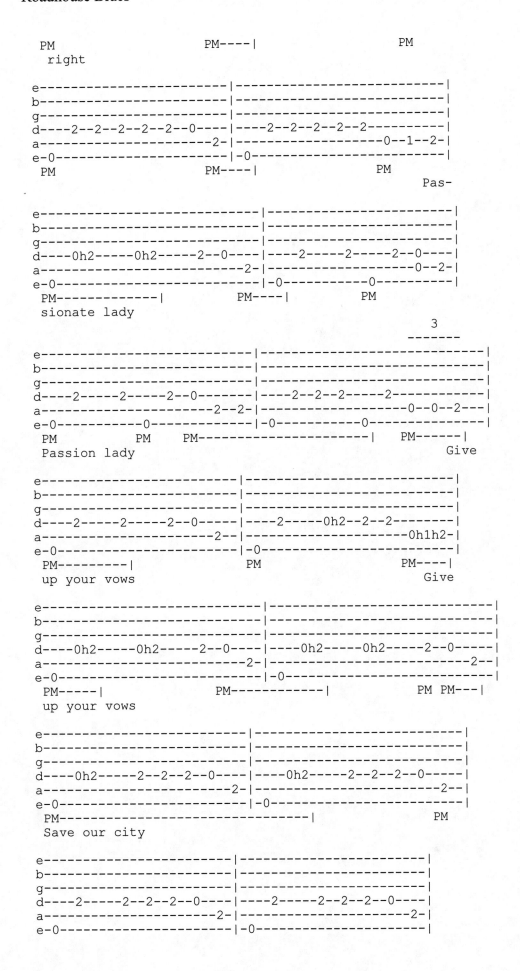

```
PM                  PM----|                    PM
Save our city                              All- right

e---------------------------|---------------------|
b---------------------------|---------------------|
g---------------------------|---------------------|
d----2-----2--2--2--0----|----2-----2-2---------|
a------------------------2-|---------------0h1/2-|
e-0-------------------------|-0-------------------|
 PM                 PM---|             PM----|
 now

e----0-----0--0-----------|----0-----0--0----------|
b----3-----3--3-----------|----3-----3--3----------|
g----1-----1--1-----------|----1-----1--1----------|
d----2-----2--2----0-1/2-|----2-----2--2----0h1/2--|
a------------2----0-----|------------2-----------|
e-0-----------0---------|-0-----------0----------|
                                            Well I

e----0---------------------|----0-----0--0----------|
b----3-----3--3-----------|----3-----3--3----------|
g----1-----1--1-----------|----1-----1--1----------|
d----2-----2--2----0-1/2---|----2-----2--2----0h1/2-|
a------------2-------------|------------2-----------|
e-0-----------0-----------|-0-----------0----------|
                         PM
 woke up this morning and I got    myself  a   beer

e----0-----0---------------|------------------------|
b----3-----3---------------|------------------------|
g----1-----1---------------|-0----------------------|
d----2-----2---------------|-0-----2p0h2-(2)p0----0----|
a---------------1--2--0h1h2-|-------------------2-----2-|
e-0------------------------|------------------------|
 PM              PM---|       PM
                                           And I

e----0-----0--0-----------|----0-----0--0----------|
b----3-----3--3-----------|----3-----3--3----------|
g----1-----1--1-----------|----1-----1--1----------|
d----2-----2--2----0h1h2---|----2-----2--2----0h1h2--|
a------------------------|------------------------|
e-0-----------------------|-0----------------------|
 PM                          PM
 woke up this morning and I got    myself  a   beer

                          |‾|-|
e----0---------------------|------------------------|
b----3-----3--------------|------------------------|
g----1-----1--------------|---0--------------------|
d----2-----2--------0h1h2--|-0------2-0h2--0-----0----|
a----------2---0--1--------|----------------0h2----2-|
e-0--------0--------------|------------------------|
 PM                                          The

e---------------------------|------------------------|
b---------------------------|------------------------|
g---------------------------|------------------------|
d-0-----0-----0--------0h2-|(2)/\/\--0-----------0--------|
a----2-----2-----2---------|-------------0h2----0--------|
e--------------------------|--------------------3/\/\-|
 future's uncertain and the end    is always    near
```

```
e----------------------------|-----------------------------|
b----------------------------|-----------------------------|
g----------------------------|-0----------X----------------|
d----------------------------|------2--0h2--(2)/\/\--2p0-|
a---------------------0h1h2-|-----------------------------|
e-(3)/\/\--0--0--0--0--------|-----------------------------|
                                                 Let it
```

```
        Outro
e----------------------|-------------------------|
b----------------------|-------------------------|
g----------------------|-------------------------|
d-------------2------4--2-|-------------2-----4--2--|
a-0--0--3--4------------|-0--0--3--4-----0--------|
e----------------------|-------------------------|
                        PM---------|   PM
  roll        baby  roll            Let it
```

```
e----------------------|-------------------------|
b----------------------|-------------------------|
g----------------------|-------------------------|
d-------------2------4--2-|-------------2-----4--2--|
a-0-----3--4-----0-------|-0--0--3--4-----0--------|
e----------------------|-------------------------|
              PM
  roll        baby  roll                Let it
```

```
e----------------------|--------------------------|
b----------------------|--------------------------|
g----------------------|--------------------------|
d-------------2------4--2-|-------------2------------|
a-0-----3--4-----0-------|-0---0-3--4-----0--4------|
e----------------------|--------------------------|
              PM
  roll        baby  roll                Let it
```

```
    3      3     3     3           3           3
   -----  -----  -----  -----     ---------   ---------
e----------------------------|-----------------------|
b-4-4-4-4-4-4-4-4-4-4-4-4-4-|-4---4---5---6---7---8-|
g-4-4-4-4-4-4-4-4-4-4-4-4-4-|-4---4---5---6---7---8-|
d-4-4-4-4-4-4-4-4-4-4-4-4-4-|-4---4---5---6---7---8-|
a-2-2-2-2-2-2-2-2-2-2-2-2-2-|-2---2---3---4---7---6-|
e----------------------------|-----------------------|
  roll                          all night
```

```
  Gtr1
|e--------------------------------------------|------------------|
|b-9------------------------------------------|------------------|
|g-9------------------------------------------|------------------|
|d-9------------------------------------------|------------------|
|a-7------------------------------------------|------------------|
|e--------------------------------------------|------------------|
|                                             |                  |
|            3                   3            |                  |
|          --------           ----------      |                  |
|Gtr2                                         |                  |
|    )                     )¯(               |                  |
|e-15-----15-12----------)--(-----------|------------------|
|b--------------15-12---)---(-----------|-------7/9-\7-----|
|g--------------------14-----(14)p12----|-12\---7/9-\7-----|
|d-------------------------------14-|-------6/8-\6-----|
```

```
|a----------------------------------------|-------7/9-\7-----|
|e----------------------------------------|-----------------|
```

Written out by The Loan Arranger
4/8/97

                    Hi Ho Silver, Away
                      The Loan Arranger

Back to The Doors list
Go Back to Chord Library
Go Back to Main

Who is burn-in'?   Who is burn-in'?   Ef-fi-gy.____

Who is burn-in'?   Who is burn-in'?   Ef-fi-gy.____

Why?   Why?   Why-y?____   Ef-fi-gy.____

Repeat and fade out

Effigy - 3 - 3

TAKE IT LIKE A FRIEND

Words and Music by
S. COOK

Take It Like A Friend - 4 - 1

Take It Like A Friend - 4 - 2

20

21

Take It Like A Friend - 4 - 4

Repeat ad lib and fade

HELLO MARY LOU

Words and Music by
GENE PITNEY

Moderato

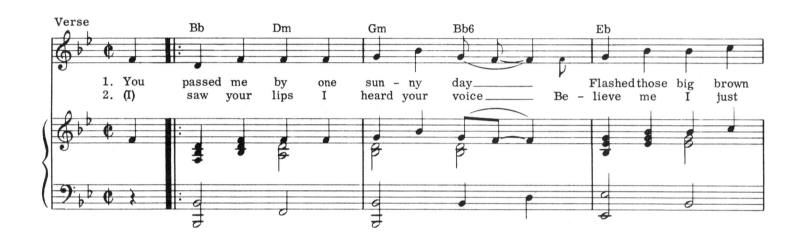

Verse

Bb   Dm   Gm   Bb6   Eb

1. You passed me by one sun-ny day_____ Flashed those big brown
2. (I) saw your lips I heard your voice_____ Be-lieve me I just

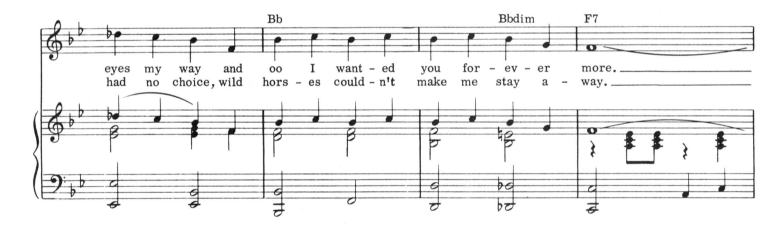

Bb   Bbdim   F7

eyes my way and oo I want-ed you for-ev-er more._____
had no choice, wild hors-es could-n't make me stay a-way._____

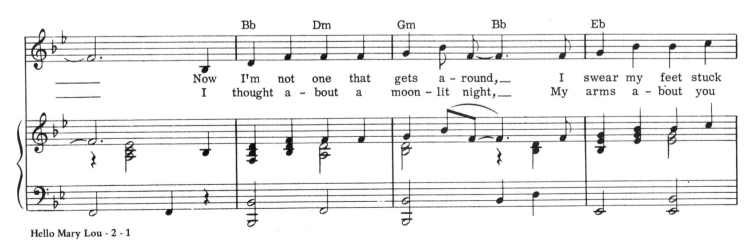

Bb   Dm   Gm   Bb   Eb

_____ Now I'm not one that gets a-round,__ I swear my feet stuck
_____ I thought a-bout a moon-lit night,__ My arms a-bout you

Hello Mary Lou - 2 - 1

CHAMELEON

J.C. FOGERTY

Moderately Bright (In Four)

You took me run - nin' up a wrong way street.

When we got there, you said, "Can't you read?"

I must be blind, but now and then I see

Chameleon - 3 - 1

25

Chameleon - 3 - 2

D. S. al ⊕ Coda 𝄋

⊕ *Coda*

Repeat ad lib. and fade

I see tri - an - gles, and you say__ it's round,__ round, round.

Saw an emp - ty glass;__ you said it's full.__

Lord, it's so__ hot, then you come__ on cool, cool.__

RAMBLE TAMBLE

J.C. FOGERTY

Ramble Tamble - 3 - 1

28

Bugs in the su - gar, Mort-gage on the home, Mort-gage on the
Po-lice on the cor -ner, Mort-gage on the car, Mort-gage on the

1.

home.   There's
car.

2.

Move,_____ down___ the

Csus   C

road   I   go.   They're

Ramble Tamble - 3 - 2

selling in-de-pen-dence, Ac-tors in the White House, Ac-id in-di-

ges-tion, Mort-gage on my life, Mort-gage on my life.

Move,_____ down___ the

road I go.

Keep repeating and fade

Ramble Tamble - 3 - 3

GLOOMY

J.C. FOGERTY

Gloomy - 2 - 1

Gloomy - 2 - 2

KEEP ON CHOOGLIN'

J.C. FOGERTY

Keep On Chooglin' - 2 - 1

You got to ball and have a good time___ And that's what I___ call Choo - gl - in'.

For Repeats | *Last time*   F7

Keep on Choog-   Keep on Choog - lin',   Keep on   Choog - lin',

Keep on Choog - lin',   Choog - lin',   Choog- lin'.

2. Here comes Mary lookin' for Harry,
   She gonna choogle tonight.
   Here comes Louie, works in the sewer,
   He gonna choogle tonight. (Chours)

3. If you can choose it, who can refuse it,
   You gotta choogle tonight.
   Go on, take your pick, right from the git go,
   Y'all be chooglin' tonight. (Chorus)

Keep On Chooglin - 2 - 2

CROSS-TIE WALKER

J.C. FOGERTY

Cross-Tie Walker - 2 - 1

TRAVELIN' BAND

J.C. FOGERTY

Travelin' Band - 3 - 1

38

NEED SOMEONE TO HOLD

D. CLIFFORD and S. COOK

Need Someone To Hold - 3 - 1

Need Someone To Hold - 3 - 3

Repeat ad lib & fade

WROTE A SONG FOR EVERYONE

J.C. FOGERTY

Wrote A Song For Everyone - 2 - 1

All I want, All I want is to write my-self a tune.
All I want, All I want is to get you down to pray.
They could have saved a mil-lion peo-ple, How can I tell you?

CHORUS

Wrote A Song For Ev-'ry-one, Wrote a song for truth. Wrote A Song For

To Coda

Ev-'ry-one_____ and I could-n't ev-en talk to you. you.

D. S. al Coda

Coda

cou- ou- ou- ou- ould- n't ev- en talk to you.

Wrote A Song For Everyone - 2 - 2

LOOKIN' OUT MY BACK DOOR

J.C. FOGERTY

Lookin' Out My Back Door - 2 - 1

Lookin' Out My Back Door - 2 - 2

BOOTLEG

J.C. FOGERTY

Moderately Bright

mf

CHORUS C7

Boot-leg, Boot - leg;   Boot-leg, Haw - da.

(Optional 8 basso throughout)

Boot-leg, Boot - leg;   Boot-leg, Haw - da.

VERSE C7

Take you a glass of wa - ter   And make it a -gainst___ the law.
Find - in' a na - tu-ral wo - man,   Like hon - ey to___ a bee.
Su - zy may-be give you some cher - ry pie,   But Lord, that ain't___ no fun.

Bootleg - 2 - 1

SOMEDAY NEVER COMES

J.C. FOGERTY

Someday Never Comes - 3 - 1

50

POORBOY SHUFFLE

J.C. FOGERTY

Medium Shuffle Tempo

Poorboy Shuffle - 3 - 1

52

Poorboy Shuffle - 3 - 2

53

Poorboy Shuffle - 3 - 3

SUSIE-Q

Words and Music by
D. HAWKINS, S.J. LEWIS
and E. BROADWATER

55

Suzie - Q - 2 - 2

GET DOWN WOMAN

J.C. FOGERTY

Get Down Woman - 2 - 1

58

RUN THROUGH THE JUNGLE

J.C. FOGERTY

Run Through The Jungle - 3 - 1

Run Through The Jungle - 3 - 2

60

Run Through The Jungle - 3 - 3

I PUT A SPELL ON YOU

Words and Music by
JAY HAWKINS

I Put A Spell On You - 3 - 1

I Put A Spell On You - 3 - 3

GREEN RIVER

J.C. FOGERTY

Moderately

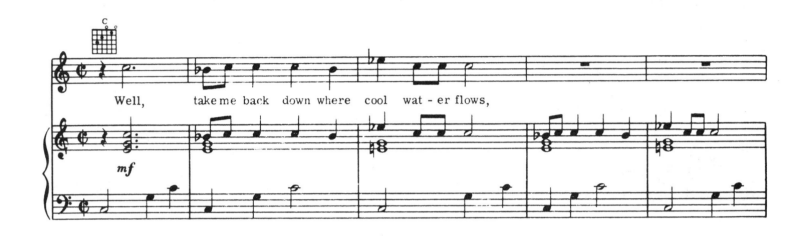

Well, take me back down where cool wat-er flows,

Let me re-mem-ber things I love, Stop-pin' at the log where

cat-fish bite, Walk-in' a-long the riv-er road at night, Bare-foot girls

Green River - 3 - 1

66

Green River - 3 - 3

DOOR TO DOOR

S. COOK

Find me out a - walk - in', time the whis - tle starts a - call - in',
Here's my lat - est sam - ple; like to show you how to use it.

May - be stop - pin' ear - ly, knock - in' at your door. Take so long to
First, you pull the cur - tain while I spread some here. Wipe the sur - face

an - swer, Lord knows it ain't the milk - man Could be stop - pin' ear - ly, sell - in'
gent - ly, try to use a cir - cle mo - tion, Safe for all your prob - lems, and my

Door To Door - 3 - 1

Door To Door - 3 - 3

SWEET HITCH-HIKER

J.C. FOGERTY

PORTERVILLE

J.C. FOGERTY

It's been an aw-ful long time since I been home, But you won't catch me go-in' back down there a-lone.

Things they said when I was young are quite e-nough to get me hung. I *don't care!* I *don't care!* They

came and took my Dad a-way to serve some time, But it was me that paid the debt he left be-hind.

Porterville - 2 - 1

THE NIGHT TIME IS THE RIGHT TIME

Words and Music by
LEW HERMAN

The Night Time Is The Right Time - 3 - 1

be with the one you love. I ____ said the

night time,__ ooh,__ is the right time__ to

be with the one you love. I said the

The Night Time Is The Right Time - 3 - 2

Verse 2:
Baby, I said a - baby, baby,
Come on and drive me crazy, Lord,
You know I love you;
Always thinkin' of you.
Hey, baby; oh, I said a - baby.
You know that night time is the
Right time to be with the one you love.

Verse 3: (Instrumental Solo)
Verse 4: (Repeat 1st Verse)

IT CAME OUT OF THE SKY

J.C. FOGERTY

It Came Out Of The Sky - 3 - 1

It Came Out Of The Sky - 3 - 3

LONG AS I CAN SEE THE LIGHT

J.C. FOGERTY

Long As I Can See The Light - 3 - 1

Long As I Can See The Light - 3 - 2

82

Long As I Can See The Light - 3 - 3

BORN ON THE BAYOU

J.C. FOGERTY

Now, when I was just— a lit - tle boy,— Stand-in' to my Dad-dy's knee,—

My pop-pa said, "Son, don't let— the man get you and do— what he done to me."

Born On The Bayou - 3 - 1

84

Born On The Bayou - 3 - 2

WALK ON THE WATER

Words and Music by
TOM FOGERTY and
J.C. FOGERTY

Walk On The Water - 2 - 1

SINISTER PURPOSE

J.C. FOGERTY

When the sky is gray and the moon is hate
Burn a-way the good-ness; You and I re-main.

I'll be down to get you. Roots of earth will shake.
Did you see the last war? Well, here I am a - gain.

Sin - is - ter Pur-pose Knock-in' at your___ door; Come and take my___

Sinister Purpose - 2 - 1

Sinister Purpose - 2 - 2

OOBY DOOBY

Words and Music by
WADE MOORE and
DICK PENNER

Ooby-Dooby - 2 - 1

Ooby-Dooby - 2 - 2

LODI

J.C. FOGERTY

Lodi - 2 - 1

FORTUNATE SON

J.C. FOGERTY

Fortunate Son - 2 - 1

Fortunate Son - 2 - 2

COTTON FIELDS

Words and Music by
HUDDIE LEDBETTER

Moderately fast

Cotton Fields - 2 - 1

2. It may sound a little funny
   But you didn't make very much money
   In them old cotton fields at home;
   It may sound a little funny
   But you didn't make very much money
   In them old cotton fields at home. (Chorus)

3. I was home in Arkansas,
   People ask me what you come here for,
   In them old cotton fields at home;
   I was home in Arkansas,
   People ask me what you come here for,
   In them old cotton fields at home. (Chorus)

Cotton Fields - 2 - 2

BEFORE YOU ACCUSE ME

Words and Music by
E. McDANIELS

1. 6. Be - fore you ac-cuse me, take a look at your - self.
2. 3. 5. *(See additional lyrics)*
4. 7. 8. *(Instrumental Solo)*

Be - fore you ac-cuse me, take a look at your-

- self. You

Before You Accuse Me - 2 - 1

say I been buy-in' oth-er wom-en clothes,— but you've been talk-in' to some - one

else.

2. I
3. Be -
5. Come

Verse 2:
I called your mama
'Bout three or four nights ago.
I called your mama
'Bout three or four nights ago.
Your mama said, "Son,
Don't call my daughter no more."

Verse 3:
Before you accuse me,
Take a look at yourself.
Before you accuse me,
Take a look at yourself.
You say I've been buyin' other women clothes,
But you've been takin' money from someone else.

Verse 4: *(Instrumental Solo)*

Verse 5:
Come on back home, baby;
Try my love one more time.
Come on back home, baby;
Try my love one more time.
You've been gone away so long,
I'm just about to lose my mind.

Verse 6: *(Repeat 1st Verse)*

Verse 7 & 8: *(Instrumental Solo)*

SAIL AWAY

S. COOK

Moderately Bright (in 4)

mf

Lock the door.— sun's a-fall-in'. Poke the fire.— don't let the cold— in. Gon-na try— to

sail a-way— from the rest of my— life. *To Coda* Found a boat— to make the break— in,

Filled with hope— 'bout the step I'm tak - in'. Gon-na try—— to sail a-way— from the

Sail Away - 3 - 1

Sail Away - 3 - 2

Sail Away - 3 - 3

Repeat ad lib and fade out

TEARIN' UP THE COUNTRY

D. CLIFFORD

1. Play- in' a pa - vil - ion on the out - skirts of town,
2. Mom and pa - pa told me "Son, you got - ta go to school;
3. Ran in - to a dry spell, _____ seemed no - where to go.

Play - in' where my roll - er der - by rolls. Just a
On - ly way to make the fam - 'ly proud." I re-
Good luck turned the tide, I'm on my way.

part- time mu - sic man, A no - bod - y at the plant, I'm
I paid no at - ten - tion, — left my_ books at home, —
mem - ber load - in' big trucks when the sum - mer_ sun was hot, You

Tearin' Up The Country - 3 - 1

Tearin' Up The Country - 3 - 2

Tearin' Up The Country - 3 - 3

THE WORKING MAN

J.C. FOGERTY

nev - er had no day off since I learned right from wrong.
Pop- pa threw m~ out. — Said, "I got - ta earn my own way."
I'm The Work ~ Man, — And I do the job for you.

INTERLUDE

2. Ma-ma I ain't nev -er been in trou- ble;

D. S. al ◈ Coda 𝄋

I ain't got__ the time.__ I don't mess a -round with mag-ic, child.__ What-

Coda

rit.

4. Every Friday, Well, that's when I get paid;
Don't take me on Friday, 'cause that's when I get paid.
Let me die on Saturday night, before Sunday gets my head.

The Working Man - 2 - 2

PROUD MARY

J.C. FOGERTY

Proud Mary - 2 - 1

VERSE

Proud Mary - 2 - 2

(Wish I Could)
HIDEAWAY

J.C. FOGERTY

How-dy, friend,_ beg-gin' your par - don,_ Is there some-thin' on your mind?

You've gone and sold_ all your be-long - ings,_ Is that some-thing in your eye? Well, I

Wish I Could Hideaway - 4 - 1

112

Wish I Could Hideaway - 4 - 3

113

Wish I Could Hideaway - 4 - 4

FEELIN' BLUE

J.C. FOGERTY

Moderately Slow

mf

VERSE D7

Hey, look o-ver yon-der out in the rain, Soak-in' wet fe-ver in my brain.

Now, I ain't cer-tain which way to go, But I got to move,_____ sure._ Feel-in'

CHORUS D7

Blue, blue, blue, blue, blue._____ Feel-in' Blue, blue, blue, blue, blue._____ Feel-in'

Feelin' Blue - 2 - 1

2. Hey, look over yonder, behind the wall, They're closin' in I'm about to fall.
   Now I'm no coward, but I ain't no fox, Feel it in my bones, my book is due.
   (Repeat Chorus)
3. Hey, look over yonder, up in the tree, There's a rope hangin' just for me.
   Without a warnin', without a warnin', Things are pilin' up to break me down.
   (Repeat Chorus)
4. Hey, look over yonder, out in the street, People laughin' by, walkin' easy.
   Now, I'm no sinner, but I ain't no saint. If it's happy, you can say I ain't.

Feelin' Blue - 2 - 2

COMMOTION

J.C. FOGERTY

Commotion - 2 - 1

THE MIDNIGHT SPECIAL

J.C. FOGERTY

The Midnight Special - 3 - 1

The Midnight Special - 3 - 2

120

The Midnight Special - 3 - 3

UP AROUND THE BEND

J.C. FOGERTY

Up Around The Bend - 3 - 1

122

Up Around The Bend - 3 - 2

Up Around The Bend - 3 - 3

PENTHOUSE PAUPER

J.C. FOGERTY

Penthouse Pauper - 2 - 1

VERSE

3. If I was a gambler, You know I'd never lose,
And if I were a guitar player, Lord, I'd have to play the blues
(Remainder of 3rd verse: Instrumental)

4. If I was a hacksaw, My blade would be razor sharp.
If I were a politician, I could prove that monkeys talk.
You can find the tallest building,
Lord, You know I'd have the house on top.

5. I'm the Penthouse Pauper; I got nothin' to my name..
I'm the Penthouse Pauper; I got nothin' to my name.
I can be most anything,
'Cause when you got nothin' it's all the same.

Penthouse Pauper - 2 - 2

MY BABY LEFT ME

Words and Music by
ARTHUR CRUDUP

Moderately Bright

Chorus:
tacet

1. Yes, my ba - by
2. stand at my
3.4.(See additional lyrics)

left me, nev - er said a word. Was it
win - dow, wring my hands and cry. I hate to

some - thing I done, some - thing that she heard? My ba - by left me,
lose that wom - an, hate to say good - bye. You know she left me,

My Baby Left Me - 2 - 1

Verse 3:
Baby, one of these mornings, Lord, it won't be long,
You'll look for me and, Baby, and Daddy he'll be gone.
You know you left me, you know you left me.
My baby even left me, never said goodbye.

Verse 4:
Now, I stand at my window, wring my hands and moan.
All I know is that the one I love is gone.
My baby left me, you know she left me.
My baby even left me, never said a word.

My Baby Left Me - 2 - 2

DOWN ON THE CORNER

J.C. FOGERTY

Down On The Corner - 2 - 1

BORN TO MOVE

J.C. FOGERTY

Born To Move - 2 - 1

Born To Move - 2 - 2

GRAVEYARD TRAIN

J.C. FOGERTY

Graveyard Train - 2 - 1

For Repeats | Last time

fade-out

2. I had some words to holler, And my Rosie took a ride.

3. In the moonlight, See the Greyhound rollin' on.

4. In the moonlight, See the Greyhound rollin' on.

5. Flyin' through the crossroads, Rosie ran into the Hound.

6. For the graveyard, Thirty boxes made of bone.

7. For the graveyard, Thirty boxes made of bone.

8. Mister Undertaker, Take this coffin from my home.

9. In the midnight, Hear my cryin' out her name.

10. In the midnight, Hear me cryin' out her name.

11. I'm standin' on the railroad, Waitin' for the Graveyard Train.

12. On the highway, Thirty people turned to stone.

13. On the highway, Thirty people turned to stone.

14. Oh, take me to the station, 'Cause I'm number thirty-one.

Graveyard Train - 2 - 2

TOMBSTONE SHADOW

J.C. FOGERTY

Tombstone Shadow - 2 - 1

VERSE 3

The man gave me a luck charm,
Cost five dollars more,
Said, "Put some on your pillow,
and put some on your door."
He said, "Take a long vacation,
for thirteen months or more."

Tombstone Shadow - 2 - 2   **REPEAT VERSE 1**

SIDE O' THE ROAD

J.C. FOGERTY

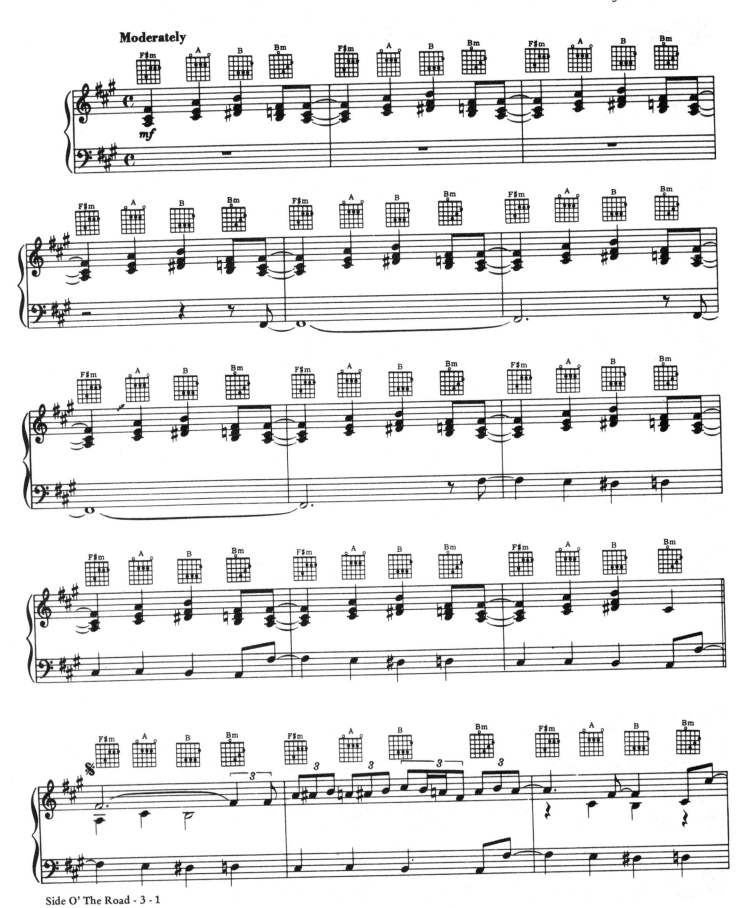

Side O' The Road - 3 - 1

Side O' The Road - 3 - 2

NINETY-NINE AND A HALF WON'T DO

Words and Music by
W. PICKETT/S. CROPPER/E. FLOYD

Moderate two beat

1. I got to have all your love,_____ night_ and
2.3.(See additional lyrics)

day.

140

Ninety-Nine And A Half Won't Do - 3 - 2

Verse 2:
Don't be led in the wrong direction.
To start this thing off right,
I may need a little love and affection,
Yes I do.
(To Chorus:)

Verse 3:
We got to bring it down,
Start gettin' it right.
We got to stop this messin' around,
And keep the thing up tight,
Yes we do, now.
(To Chorus:)

Ninety-Nine And A Half Won't Do - 3 - 3

IT'S JUST A THOUGHT

J.C. FOGERTY

It's Just A Thought - 3 - 1

144

It's Just A Thought - 3 - 3

GOOD GOLLY MISS MOLLY

Words and Music by
ROBERT BLACKWELL
and JOHN MARASCALCO

Good Gol - ly Miss Mol - ly, Yeah you sure__ like a ball,__

Well, Good Gol - ly Miss Mol - ly, Yeah you sure like a ball.____

When you're shak - in' and a shout - in' Can't you hear__ your Mom - ma call?

Good Golly Miss Molly - 3 - 1

146

Good Golly Miss Molly - 3 - 3

HAVE YOU EVER SEEN THE RAIN?

J.C. FOGERTY

Have You Ever Seen The Rain? - 3 - 1

VERSE

Yes- ter-day, and days—— be-fore,—— Sun is cold and rain—— is hard,—— I know;——

Been that way—— for all—— my time.—— 'Til for-ev - er, on—— it goes——

Through the cir-cle, fast—— and slow,—— I know;—— And it can't stop,—— I won - der.

D. S. al ✦ Coda

⊕Coda

WHO'LL STOP THE RAIN

J.C. FOGERTY

Who'll Stop The Rain - 3 - 1

Good men through the ag - es, Tryin' to find the
Five year plans and new deals,_ Wrapped in gold - en

sun; And I won - der, Still I won - der, Who'll Stop The Rain._
chains.

1. **2.**

Heard the sing - ers play - in',_ How we cheered_ for more. The

Who'll Stop The Rain - 3 - 2

Who'll Stop The Rain - 3 - 3

MOLINA

J.C. FOGERTY

Moderately Bright (In Four)

Mo - li - i - i - i - na, where you go - in' to? Mo-

li - i - i - i - na, where you go - in' to? She's

daugh-ter to the may - or, Mess-in' with the sher - iff, Driv-in' in a blue car, She don't see no red light. Mo-

155

Molina - 3 - 2

156

DON'T LOOK NOW

By
J. C. FOGERTY

Who will take the coal from the mine?
Who will work the coal field with his hands?

Who will take the salt from the earth?
Who will put his back to the plough?

Who'll _____ take a leaf and grow it to a tree?
Who'll _____ take the moun - tain and give it to the sea?

Don't Look Now - 3 - 1

158

Don't Look Now, it ain't you or me.

me. Don't Look Now, some-one's done your

star - vin';_____ Don't Look Now, some-one's done your

pray - in' too. Who will make the shoes for your
Who will take the coal from the

Don't Look Now - 3 - 3

(Theme From)
RUDE AWAKENING NO. 2

J.C. FOGERTY

Theme From Rude Awakening 2 - 3 - 1

Theme From Rude Awakening 2 - 3 - 2

162

Theme From Rude Awakening 2 - 3 - 3

39635

HEY, TONIGHT

J.C. FOGERTY

Hey, Tonight - 3 - 1

164

Hey, Tonight - 3 - 2

LOOKIN' FOR A REASON

J.C. FOGERTY

168

Lookin' For A Reason - 3 - 3   *Fade out on repeat of Chorus*

I HEARD IT THROUGH THE GRAPEVINE

Words and Music by
NORMAN WHITFIELD
and BARRETT STRONG

SUPERSTARS OF AMERICAN POP

BEST OF CREEDENCE CLEARWATER REVIVAL
___ (P0700SMX)

This piano/vocal/chords edition features 18 of Creedence Clearwater Revival's greatest songs. Fake arrangements of each tune are provided also. Contents include: Bad Moon Rising ● Proud Mary ● Have You Ever ● Who'll Stop The Rain ● Born On The Bayou and more.

CREEDENCE CLEARWATER REVIVAL / COMPLETE
___ (P0408SMX)

Arranged for piano/vocal/chords, this collection contains 65 songs. Contents include: I Put A Spell On You ● Suzie Q ● Born On The Bayou ● Proud Mary ● Green River ● Bad Moon Rising ● Lodi ● Down On The Corner ● Fortunate Son ● Who'll Stop The Rain ● Travelin' Band ● Lookin' Out My Back Door ● Have You Ever Seen The Rain? ● Hey, Tonight ● Sweet Hitch-Hiker and many more.

THE DOORS COMPLETE
___ (P0443SMX)

The Doors: the legendary group of the late 60's who helped usher in the era of self-awareness. Mystical Jim Morrison captured the imagination of America's youth. This piano/vocal/chords folio recaptures it all with great music including: The Crystal Ship ● L.A. Woman ● Break On Through ● Riders On The Storm ● Runnin' Blues ● The Soft Parade ● Touch Me and Wishful Sinful.

THE DOORS GREATEST HITS
___ (P0442SMX)

Arranged for piano/vocal/chords, this matching songbook features the same great songs recorded on the album. Rekindle the memories with ten of The Doors biggest hits, including: Light My Fire ● Hello, I Love You ● People Are Strange ● Love Me Two Times and more.

BEST OF THE BEACH BOYS
___ (P0675SMX)

Enjoy these ever-popular songs made famous by The Beach Boys. This piano/vocal/chords collection includes 18 top hits such as: Help Me Rhonda ● California Girls ● Fun, Fun, Fun ● I Get Around ● Surfer Girl ● Wouldn't It Be Nice and more. Join in the fun!

THE BEST OF THE BEACH BOYS

PIANO/VOCAL/CHORDS

All Summer Long	Fun, Fun, Fun	Little Deuce Coupe
Barbara Ann	Getcha Back	Shut Down
California Girls	Girls On The Beach	Surfer Girl
Catch A Wave	Help Me Rhonda	Surfin'
Do It Again	I Get Around	Surfin' Safari
409	In My Room	Surfin' U.S.A.
		Wouldn't It Be Nice

THE BEACH BOYS COMPLETE — Vol. 1
___ (P0413SMX)

Over 70 songs made famous by The Beach Boys! Arranged for piano/vocal/chords, the songs include: Help Me Rhonda ● Surfin' Safari ● Little Deuce Coupe ● California Girls ● Barbara Ann ● I Get Around ● Wendy ● Don't Worry Baby ● Wouldn't It Be Nice ● Fun, Fun, Fun ● In My Room ● When I Grow Up (To Be A Man) ● 409 ● All Summer Long and more!

THE BEST OF THE FOUR TOPS
___ (P0774SMX)

In this successful "Best Of" Series, enjoy memorable songs from the 60's! The sixteen titles include: Baby I Need Your Loving ● Bernadette ● I Can't Help Myself (Sugar Pie, Honey Bunch) ● It's The Same Old Song ● 7 Rooms Of Gloom ● Shake Me ● Wake Me (When It's Over).

THE BEST OF THE FOUR TOPS

	PIANO/VOCAL/CHORDS	
Ask The Lonely	Loving You Is Sweeter Than Ever	Standing In The Shadows Of Love
Baby I Need Your Loving	Reach Out I'll Be There	Still Water (Love)
Bernadette	7 Rooms	What Is A Man?

THE BEST OF THE SUPREMES
___ (P0771SMX)

These songs live on through the decades! Play and sing such timeless hits as Baby Love ● Come See About Me ● I Hear A Symphony ● My World Is Empty Without You ● Stop! In The Name Of Love ● Someday We'll Be Together ● You Can't Hurry Love and Love Child.

THE BEST OF THE SUPREMES

	PIANO/VOCAL/CHORDS	
Baby Love	Love Child	Reflections
Back In My Arms Again	Love Is Here And Now You're Gone	Someday We'll Be Together
Come See About Me	My World Is Empty Without You	Stop! In The Name Of Love
The Happening	Nothing But Heartaches	You Can't Hurry Love
I Hear A Symphony		You Keep Me Hangin' On
In And Out Of Love		

THE BEST OF THE TEMPTATIONS
___ (P0772SMX)

Contains these hit songs: Ain't Too Proud To Beg ● Cloud Nine ● Get Ready ● Just My Imagination (Running Away With Me) ● My Girl and Papa Was A Rolling Stone.